Vilnius Travel Highlights

Best Attractions & Experiences

Nicole Rhodes

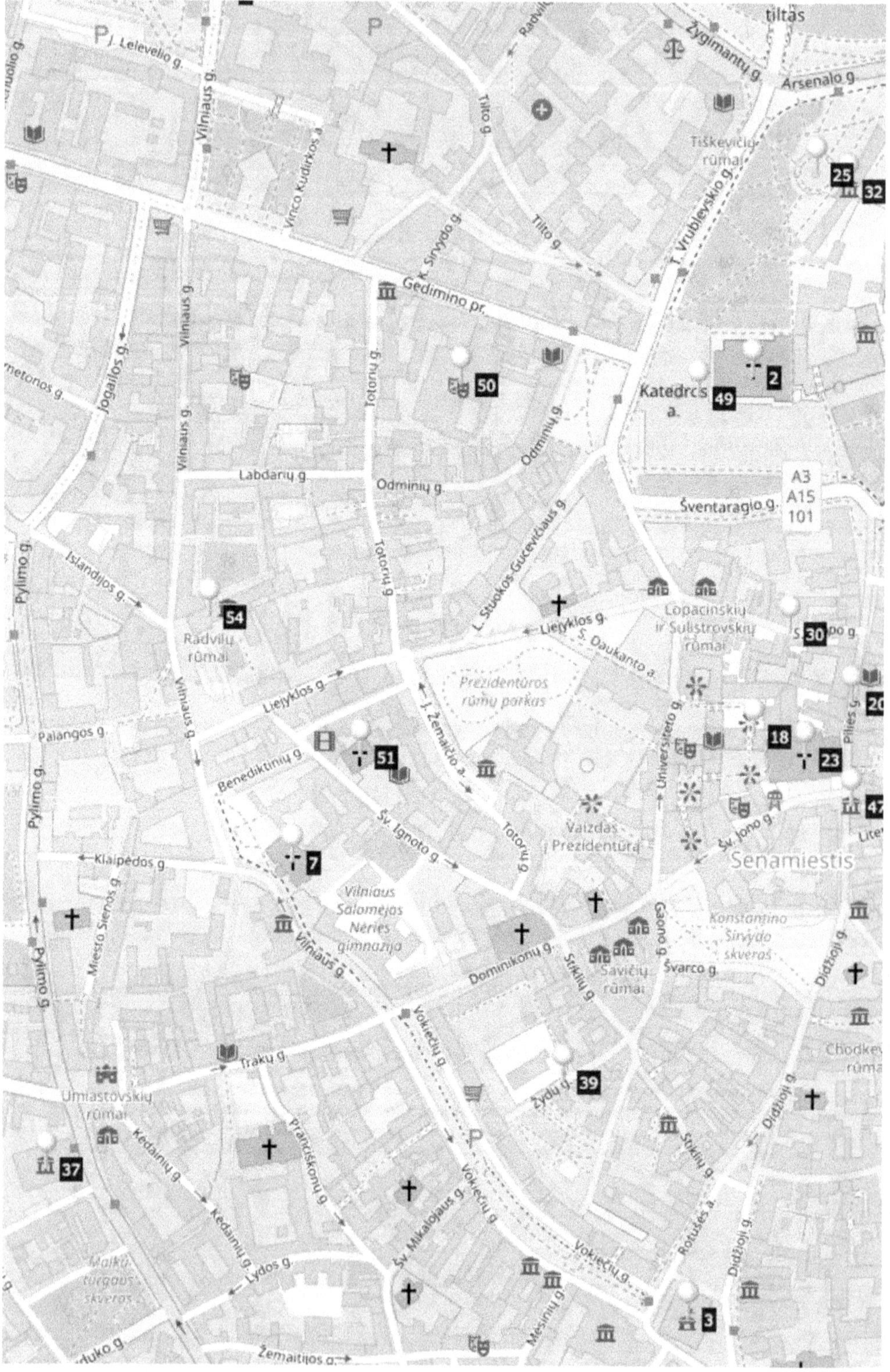

tiltas
J. Lelevelio g.
Žygimantų g.
Arsenalo g.
Tiškevičių rūmai
25
32
K. Sirvydo g.
Tilto g.
Gedimino pr.
Vinco Kudirkos g.
50
Katedros a.
49
2
Labdarių g.
Odminių g.
Šventaragio g.
A3
A15
101
Nemetonos g.
Jogailos g.
Islandijos g.
Totorių g.
L. Stuokos-Gucevičiaus g.
Lietyklos g.
Lopacinskių ir Sulistrovskių rūmai
S. Daukanto a.
30
54
Radvilų rūmai
Prezidentūros rūmų parkas
20
Palangos g.
Vilniaus g.
Lietyklos g.
J. Žemaitės a.
18
23
Pylimo g.
Benediktinių g.
51
Totorių g.
Universiteto g.
47
7
Vaizdas į Prezidentūrą
Šv. Jono g.
Senamiestis
Klaipėdos g.
Miesto Sienos g.
Vilniaus Salomėjas Nėries gimnazija
Vilniaus g.
Dominikonų g.
Stiklių g.
Gaono g.
Konstantino Sirvydo skveras
Didžioji g.
Šv. Ignoto g.
Savičių rūmai
Švarco g.
Traku g.
Žydų g.
39
Chodke rūma
Umiastovskių rūmai
Kėdainių g.
Pranciškonų g.
P
37
Kėdainių g.
Lydos g.
Žydų g.
Vokiečių g.
Rotušės a.
Stiklių g.
Didžioji g.
Malkų turgaus skveras
Šv. Mikalojaus g.
Mėsinių g.
Vokiečių g.
3
Auko g.
Žemaitijos g.

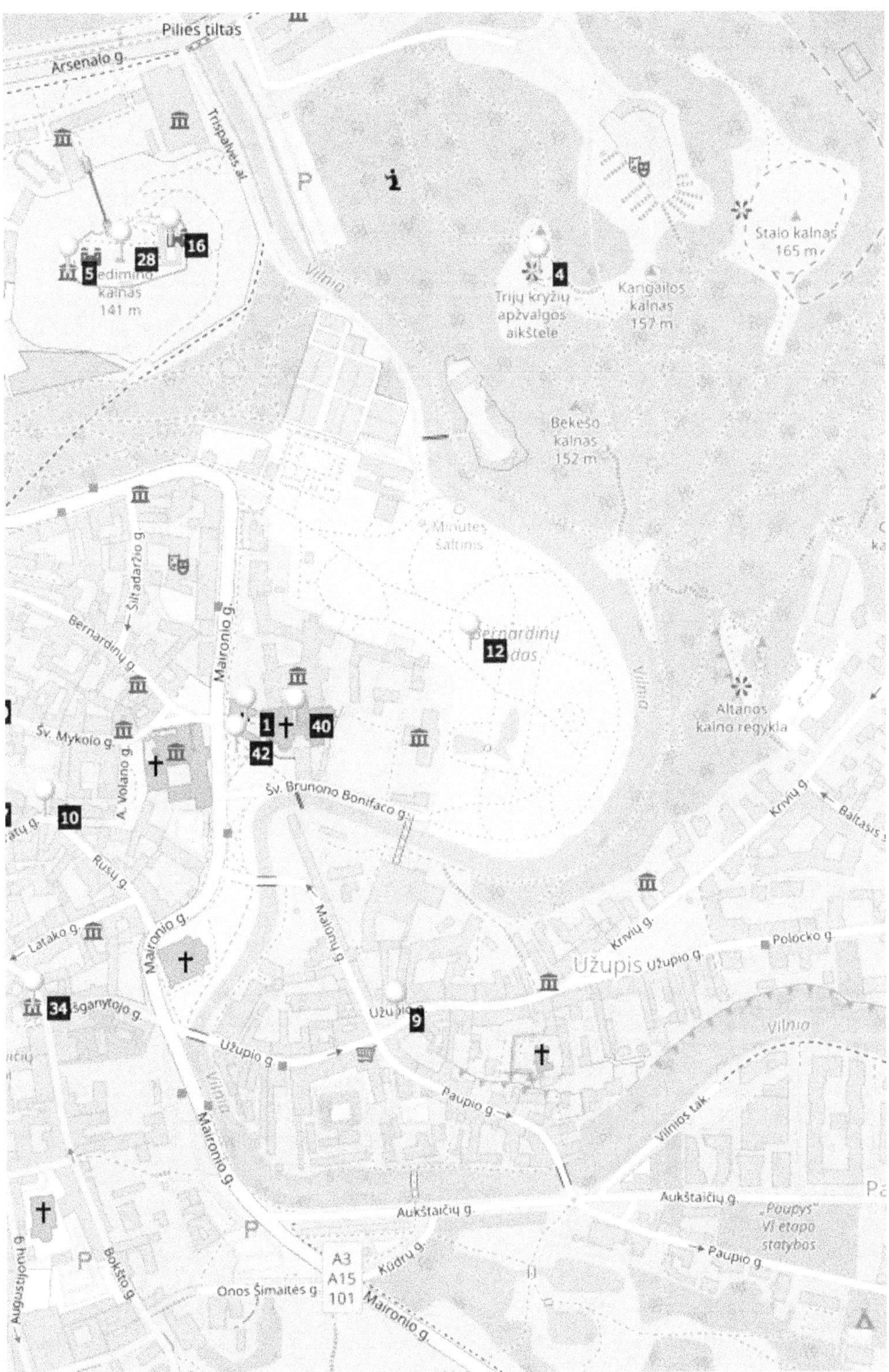

Pilies tiltas
Arsenalo g.
Trispalvės al.
P
i
Stalo kalnas 165 m
28
16
5
Gedimino kalnas 141 m
4
Trijų kryžių apžvalgos aikštelė
Kangailos kalnas 157 m
Bekešo kalnas 152 m
Minutės šaltinis
Šiltadaržio g.
Maironio g.
Bernardinų g.
Bernardinų sodas
12
Altanos kalno regykla
Vilnia
Šv. Mykolo g.
1
40
42
A. Volano g.
Šv. Brunono Bonifaco g.
10
Rusų g.
Malonų g.
Krivių g.
Baltasis
Krivių g.
Polocko g.
Lataka g.
Maironio g.
Užupis
Užupio g.
34
Išganytojo g.
9
Vilnia
Užupio g.
Vilnia
Paupio g.
Vilnios tak.
Vilnios tak.
Aukštaičių g.
Aukštaičių g.
"Paupys" VI etapo statybos
P
Paupio g.
A3
A15
101
Onos Šimaitės g.
Kudrų g.
Maironio g.
Bokšto g.
P
Suokalnio g.

Contents

Welcome to Vilnius

Lithuania's modern capital, Vilnius was once the largest city in the Baltic States. Today, extravagant buildings erected for the aristocracy during the Baroque era line its medieval cobblestone Old Town. A gateway to Eastern Europe, Vilnius offers inspiring art galleries, heritage cuisine and contemporary architecture.

☐ 1. St. Anne's Church

Address: Maironio g. 8-1, 01124 Vilnius, Lithuania

Phone: +370 67 67 44 63

Email: onosbaznycia@gmail.com

Web: http://www.onosbaznycia.lt/

St. Anne's Church in Vilnius stands on a high bank of the Vilnia River. It is a fine example of Gothic architecture, with its tower rising over the skyline of the surrounding buildings. The church is also made from bricks, which was a rare technique when it was built. Each brick in the church is decorated with intricate carvings that lend additional artistic quality to the distinctive brickwork on many surfaces. This decorative feature places St. Anne's among the oldest surviving brick churches in Lithuania.

☐ 2. Vilnius Cathedral

Address: Šventaragio g., Vilnius 01143, Lithuania
Phone: +370 5 261 0731
Email: parapija@katedra.lt
Web: http://www.katedra.lt/

The Cathedral Basilica of St Stanislaus and St Ladislaus of Vilnius is the main Roman Catholic Cathedral of Lithuania. It is situated in the heart of the Old Town, just off Cathedral Square. Dedicated to Saints Stanislaus and Ladislaus, it is the centre of Catholic spiritual life in Lithuania.

Built in the late 14th century by Gediminas, this church has been through a lot. It's been a cathedral and since 1523 and the unification of Lithuania with Poland, the coronations of its Grand Dukes took place within its confines. It became the epicenter of Catholicism in Lithuania and was the headquarters for all Catholic orders. Today, it is one of the best preserved Gothic churches in all of Eastern Europe.

☐ 3. Vilnius Town Hall

The building was designed by the Italian architect Vincenzo Michetti and built in 1848–1851 after the designs of K. E. Guzman in the Neogothic style. The Town Hall is usually considered as an example of 19th century Gothic Revival architecture. According to some opinions the Vilnius Town Hall is one of the most beautiful town halls in Eastern and Central Europe (together with Riga, Tallinn and Kaunas Town Hall).

☐ 4. The Hill of the Three Crosses

Address: Vilnius 01025, Lithuania

A fascinating religious landmark in Vilnius is the Hill of Three Crosses, which is a hill ornamented with three wooden crosses that is believed to be the burial place of seven Franciscan friars who were killed here by anti-religious forces. According to a legend, this site was used by Prussian soldiers as practice range for archery during World War II; the soldiers allegedly used the feet of executed friars as targets. This haunting site continues to inspire both locals and visitors.

☐ 5. Gediminas Tower

Address: Arsenalo g. 5, Vilnius, Lithuania
Phone: 8 5 261 74 53
Email: pilis@lnm.lt
Web: http://www.lnm.lt/

The Gediminas Tower (Lithuanian: Gedimino tornas) is the remaining part of the Upper Castle in Vilnius. The first wooden fortifications were built by , Grand Duke of Lithuania and were rebuilt at the end of the 14th century. In the 15th century, under the rule of Vytautas the Great, a brick castle was built on top of the existing fortifications; this castle was further expanded in 1423–1424 during the construction of its bastions.

□ 6. Vilniaus Street

Address: 6 Vilniaus gatvė, Vilnius 01013, Lithuania

Vilniaus street is one of the oldest streets in Vilnius. At present, it is a pedestrian street connecting old and new parts of the Old Town of Vilnius. The street is lined with 16th-19th century buildings. It has been called by different names through time: Komedija (The Building of Lithuanian Theater in the early 19th century), Cankerijos (Street of Surgical Instruments in the mid-19th century) and Kundzinskio after the merchant K. Jundzinskis (in the late 19th and early 20th centuries).

☐ 7. St Catherine's Church

Address: Vilniaus g. 30, Vilnius 01119, Lithuania
Phone: +370 5 212 2913

The Church of St. Catherine in Vilnius' Old Town is one of the most interesting religious, historical and architectural monuments. The church was built between 1618 and 1643 by Hetman and voivode of Vilnius Jan Karol Chodkiewicz as a votive church for his victory over the Swedes in the Battle of Klushino. After the death of Chodkiewicz, his heart, which had been cleansed from blood, was placed in a silver box at the top of the church tower. The box disappeared in 1813.

☐ 8. Artillery Bastion

Phone: +370 (5) 261 21 49

The Vilnius city wall was constructed between 1503 and 1522. Originally it stretched around the very center of Vilnius, the Gate of Dawn (Porta Capo), some wooden fortifications built on Birutė Hill were later incorporated into the city wall system. The main purpose of the wall was to defend the city from attacks by Crimean Tatars, in which role it played successfully in 1539 and 1655. It was also used as a source of building material during a period from the end of 17th century until mid 18th century when there were no military threats.

☐ 9. Angel of Užupis

Address: Užupio g. 14, Vilnius, Lithuania

The statue is the symbol of the freedom of art and people – the freedom with no government influence. The creator, the artist Antanas Žmuidzinavičius , wanted to reflect the idea, that Užupis is a state of a higher level, which gives citizenship only to those born within its borders. The statue, created by sculptor Antanas Žmuidzinavičius, has become an indispensable part not only of Užupis but also of Vilnius. People say that walking around it in a circle will bring them good luck.

☐ 10. Literatu Street Artwork

Address: 4 Literatų gatvė, Vilnius 01125, Lithuania

Web: https://www.facebook.com/literatugatve.lt

Web: http://www.literatugatve.lt/

Literatu, in Lithuanian means "writers" and here every writer or artist has an artwork mounted on the wall. The idea of displaying mementos of writers in public places was brought to life by a group of Lithuanian authors and artists. Authors like Jonas Biliunas, Vincentas Dargis, Gabrielius Landsbergis-Zemgulis, Czeslaw Milosz, Julija Rimkute, Tomas Venclova, and others were inspired by this idea.

☐ 11. Museum of Occupations and Freedom Fights

Address: Aukų Str. 2A, Vilnius, Lithuania

Phone: +370 5 249 62 64

Email: muziejus@genocid.lt

Web: http://genocid.lt/muziejus/

The Museum of Occupations and Freedom Fights chronologically documents the liquidation of the Lithuanian State, the establishment of Soviet rule and occupation, people's resistance against the occupation regime, deportations, genocide against the Lithuanian nation during World War II, and the period of mass repressions in Lithuania. The museum attempts to present a full picture of the years between 1940-1953 through photos, texts in different languages, sounds and videos. Exhibits document methods of torture, various methods of executions and repression against people who spoke out against the occupation or resisted it in any way.

☐ 12. Bernardine Garden

Address: Vilnius LT-2001, Lithuania

Phone: +370 5 261 1037

The Bernardine Garden is a secular park. Part of its territory is occupied by the Bernardine Monastery district and the reconstructed Gediminas Tower. Currently, it offers several exhibitions of Lithuanian art, a fish pond, fountain, statues and many more. The Bernardine Garden began to be established in 1860. This piece of land was granted for this purpose by the authorities of the Russian Empire to the Bernardinai Monastery community (of which in that time were no monks). And now, on this site there is the monastery exposition with individual buildings and landscaped gardens.

☐ 13. Egg

Address: 43 Pylimo gatvė, Vilnius 01013, Lithuania

Sitting atop a nest that is almost as big as itself, this gigantic egg in Vilnius is hard to miss. An egg-shaped bus stop that looks like an ostrich egg has become a popular meeting point for residents and tourists alike. The egg sits on the wall of Vilnius Old Town, near the Gediminas Castle. The egg itself was created by Lithuanian artist Arvydas Každailis - he wanted to represent its rich culture and heritage to tourists. The bus stop is basically used by children and dwellers of this old town during weekends.

☐ 14. Tauras Hill

Address: 5 V. Mykolaičio-Putino gatvė, Vilnius 03001, Lithuania

It is a hill in Vilnius, the capital of Lithuania. It is part of a larger official park and is located to the east of Antakalnis eldership, just west of Aleksotas elderate. The name comes from "tauras" or taura hill. The Hill has become a symbol of Vilnius and for decades has been a place where people gather for festivities, mass demonstrations and other purposes.

☐ 15. Church of St. Peter & St. Paul

Address: Antakalnio g. 1, Vilnius 10312, Lithuania
Phone: +370 5 234 0229
Email: ppbaznycia@gmail.com

The Church of St. Peter and St. Paul was built in 1507–1521 by the Italian architect Francesco Castelli, upon order of Gediminas, Grand Duke of Lithuania, as a monastery church for the Order of the Lateran (a branch of the Canons Regular). The spacious interior is unique for the exceptional richness of its sculptural decor which completely fills its three-aisle hall. Giovanni Pietro Perti created the stuccoes, Giovanni Maria Galli - painted pictures on them.

□ 16. Upper Castle

Address: Vilnius 01013, Lithuania

Built on a small hill, the present Vilnius Castle was completed in 1413. It is a complex of three castles: the Upper, Lower and Crooked. All three were reconstructed several times. The most recent reconstruction (2000–2002), led by the Spanish architect Juan Beltrán de Heredia, was abandoned when Lithuanian independence was restored. Visitors to Vilnius can also see renaissance fortifications and bastions that surround the Upper Castle; these structures date back to the 16th century.

☐ 17. Basilian Gates

Address: Aušros Vartų str. 7, Vilnius, Lithuania
Phone: +370 5 212 2578

The Basilian Gate, also known as the New Gate, was built at the northern end of Vokiečių Street (after its historic name Vilniaus gatvė) in 1761. It is a Rococo design by the Italian architect Francesco Caratti and was commissioned by the Polish-Lithuanian magnate count Stanisław Poniatowski. For a long period of time it was the only Rococo gate in Vilnius. Since 1916 it has been used by the tsarist Russian consulate and since 1944 by the Soviet consulate.

☐ 18. Vilnius University

Address: 3 Universiteto St, Vilnius, Lithuania

Phone: +370 5 268 7001

Email: infor@cr.vu.lt

Web: http://www.vu.lt/en

Vilnius University (Lithuanian: Vilniaus universitetas) is the oldest university in the Baltic states and one of the oldest state universities in Northern Europe. It is the largest university in Lithuania. It was founded in 1579 as the Jesuit Academy and was renamed "Academia et Universitas Vilnensis" when Lithuania regained its independence in 1918. The university has eight faculties, enrolls students from all over Lithuania and benefits from a worldwide network of partner institutions.

☐ 19. White Bridge

Address: 6 Upės gatvė, Vilnius 09020, Lithuania

A historical bridge in Vilnius that crosses the Neris River. Its name is derived from the color of its limestone construction. This pedestrian and bicycle bridge is also a popular spot for locals to enjoy the view of the city's old town district during festivals and other activities, including concerts at night. It was also featured on postage stamps, which has made it popular with tourists who collect postage stamps.

☐ 20. Pilies Street

Address: 15 Pilies gatvė, Vilnius 01123, Lithuania

Pilies street is one of the main streets in the Old Town of Vilnius. It is a rather short street, running from Cathedral Square to the Town Hall Square. Despite its name, it is not the widest nor the most important street in Vilnius. Still, it is very popular and crowded with tourists and locals, alike.

The natural advantage of Pilies street over the town hall square is that it is generally busier. This is largely because the street hosts artisan booths which are traditionally busy places where masses flock to buy souvenir knick-knacks.

☐ 21. Parliament of the Republic of Lithuania

Address: Gedimino avenue 53, Vilnius, Lithuania

Phone: +370 5 23 96 060

Email: priim@lrs.lt

Wikipedia: https://en.wikipedia.org/wiki/Seimas

The Parliament is the supreme representative and legislative authority of the Republic of Lithuania. It has 141 members, elected for a four-year term by proportional representation with a 5% threshold. The sessions of the Parliament are public, unless otherwise decided by a majority of its constitutional composition in secret ballot. The Seimas also performs other functions stipulated in the Constitution (e.g. adopting a declaration of war, making peace, abdication of the President and proclamation of an election).

☐ 22. Orthodox Church of the Holy Spirit

Address: Aušros Vartų gatvé 8, Vilnius, Lithuania
Phone: +370 5 212 7765

The Orthodox Church of the Holy Spirit is a Russian Orthodox church in Vilnius, rebuilt 1749–1753 in the Vilnian Baroque style. It should not be confused with the Roman Catholic Church of the Holy Spirit. Located on the right bank of Neris River, it is notable for its dome and unique belfry with tent roof on four pillars. The interior features frescoes by famous Polish-Lithuanian painter Kazimierz Wojniakowski and architect Laurynas Gucevičius.

☐ 23. St. Johns' Church

Address: Sv. Jono gatvé 12, Vilnius, Lithuania
Phone: +370 5 261 1795
Web: http://www.jonai.lt/

The Church of St. Johns dominates the ensemble of the medieval Old Town, which is consisted of medieval Orthodox and Catholic churches, convents and monasteries as well as other religious buildings. It was first mentioned in the year 1322; however it has been rebuilt several times over the years. The church is now is one of the most important sights in Vilnius Old Town and an ideal location for concerts, art exhibitions, as well as meetings with people from all around the world.

☐ 24. Rasu Cemetery

Address: Sukilėlių gatvė, Vilnius 11013, Lithuania

Rasos Cemetery in Vilnius covers an area of 10.8 hectares located in the Rasai district of old Vilnius. It is believed to be one of the most famous cemeteries in Lithuania. Established in 1805 as a graveyard for two churches near the center of town, it was later expanded in 1812.

☐ 25. King Mindaugas Memorial

Address: 1 Arsenalo gatvė, Vilnius 01143, Lithuania

Mindaugas was the first known Grand Duke of Lithuania and the only Christian King of Lithuania. Little is known of his origins, early life, or rise to power; he is mentioned in a 1219 treaty as an elder duke, and in 1236 as the leader of all the Lithuanians. The contemporary and modern sources discussing his ascent mention strategic marriages along with banishment or murder of his rivals.

☐ 26. Jewish Museum

Address: Pamėnkalnio gatvé 12, Vilnius, Lithuania
Phone: +370852620730
Email: jewishmuseum@jmuseum.lt
Web: http://www.jmuseum.lt/

The Vilna Gaon Jewish State Museum is situated on Benešovská Street in the old Jewish quarter of Vilnius. The museum's collection includes a diverse array of ritual objects, art works and books documenting Lithuanian Jewish history and culture from the 17th century to the present. These artefacts reflect the unique contribution that Lithuanian Jews made to their own communities and to wider European culture particularly in such fields as education, scholarship, trade, commerce, science and medicine. The museum also houses a collection of archival materials relating to Jewish communities in Lithuania.

☐ 27. Frank Zappa Memorial

Address: 3 K. Kalinausko gatvė, Vilnius 03107, Lithuania

The Frank Zappa Memorial, Vilnius is a statue erected in memory of the American musician Frank Zappa. It was formerly a Soviet era monument to Lenin.

☐ 28. Gediminas Hill

Address: Vilnius 01013, Lithuania

Climb the legendary Gediminas Hill near Old Town, and you'll discover a range of historical sites, superb views over the city and the river, and a fascinating insight into one of the most important periods in Lithuania's history. After passing through the Gate of Dawn (Aušros Vartai), stroll amongst one of Vilnius' most significant attractions. The Observatory terrace is a popular meeting place for locals, while other historic buildings include St Anne's Church, the Chapel of St Casimir, and the Cathedral.

☐ 29. Vingis Park

Address: Vilnius 03001, Lithuania
Web: http://www.vilniausparkai.lt/

The Vingis Park is a well-known recreational venue in Vilnius. It features a beautiful landscaped area with paths for walking and biking, the largest river in Vilnius, an amphitheater, numerous sports fields and courts, a botanical garden to be enjoyed by the locals and tourists alike, a restaurant at the river to enjoy snacks with your loved ones sitting by the river watching the boats sail down it. The park is enjoyable especially in the summer as it has multiple outdoor bars and cafes that you can enjoy while sitting under huge shade trees.

☐ 30. Skapo Street

Address: 8 S. Skapo gatvė, Vilnius 01122, Lithuania

During the first years of Skapo, the narrowest street in Vilnius was a perfect place for entertainment, but after the 19th century it became a neglected and forgotten space. Skapo district residents created «Skapo Street» project in 2011 by which the alley has been renovated and now it is a creative space with food trucks' platform, cozy coffee shop and green area.

☐ 31. Bernardinai Cemetery

Address: 15 Žvirgždyno gatvė, Vilnius 01205, Lithuania

The Bernardine Cemetery, commonly known as Užupis Cemetery is one of three oldest cemeteries in Vilnius. The cemetery covers about 38,000 square meters and has more than 14 thousand burial sites. It was established by the Bernardine monks of the Church of St. Francis of Assisi in 1810, just east of the city center in the Užupis district, and is situated on an embankment of the Vilnia river.

☐ 32. National Museum of Lithuania

Address: Arsenalo gatvé 1, Vilnius, Lithuania
Phone: +370 (5) 262 94 26
Email: informacija@lnm.lt
Web: http://www.lnm.lt/

Located in the heart of Vilnius, the National Museum is a great place to discover Lithuania's history. Explore some of our permanent displays and archeological digs. Enjoy interactive activities and experience hands-on exhibits. Visitors of all ages will enjoy exploring the museum grounds and seeing some of our unique exhibits such as the Castle of the Grand Dukes, Garden Pavilion and Blackhead House. The National Museum of Lithuania is home to many unique historic structures. The largest is the Artillery Barracks built during the reign of King August the Strong in 1710 for his personal guard regiment. It also houses a popular cafe and restaurant.

☐ 33. Verkiai Palace

Perched on a wooded slope above the Neris River, Verkiai Palace was once a favorite country retreat of the Vilnius Court. An easy walk from the old city, Verkiai Palace is surrounded by 8 hectares (20 acres) of lush gardens filled with ancient trees and fragrant roses that will delight gardeners and art lovers alike. In addition to hosting public concerts, lectures and exhibitions, Verkiai Palace houses an educational center, which offers daily activities for visitors.

☐ 34. Vilnius Art Museum

Address: Str. Bokšto 5, Vilnius, Lithuania

Phone: +370852628030

Email: muziejus@ldm.lt

Web: https://www.ldm.lt/

The Vilnius Art Museum was originally established in 1933 as the Vilnius City Museum. Its collection began with works by 19th- and 20th-century Lithuanian artists that were confiscated from private collections or purchased from artists by the museum's founder and first director, Juozas Kalinauskas, and its first curator, Vincas Krėvė-Mickevičius. In 1940, the Lithuanian Art Museum was incorporated into the Vilnius Fine Arts Museum, which had been formed that same year by merging the State Fine Arts Museum and the State Departmental Art Museum.

☐ 35. TV Tower

Address: Sausio 13-osios g. 10, Vilnius 04347, Lithuania

Phone: +370 5 25 25 333

Email: tvbokstas@telecentras.lt

The Vilnius TV Tower is a 326.5 m high tower in the Karoliniškės microdistrict of Vilnius. It is the tallest structure in Lithuania (surpassing even that of the Radiocentras building) and is occupied by the SC Lithuanian Radio and Television Centre, including a visitor's ground floor and floors 54–58. The first stage of the building was completed in 1973 and it transmitted regular TV shows starting in 1974. At that time it was just 163 m tall.

□ 36. Geographical midpoint of Europe

Address: Golfo gatvė, 15010, Lithuania

In ancient times the sources of European rivers were regarded as the centres of Europe. In the 19th century the geographical centre was calculated to be near one of the Baltic islands, and many towns claimed this title. Later in the 20th century, the centre was moved to somewhere in Eastern Europe. The candidate cities for the geographical centre of Europe have often also been considered for other titles related to their location in a particular region, such as economic and cultural capital or Green Capital.

☐ 37. MO Museum

Web: https://mo.lt/

MO museum is a modern art collection on a scale that is unprecedented in Lithuania. The museum was founded by

Dr. Danguolė Butkienė and the scientist Kęstutis Jucevičius as an alternative to Lithuanian museums, the idea being that its artworks should be accessible to all. This unique collection of over five thousand pieces includes major Lithuanian art works from the 1950s to this day as well as classics of Western European Avant-Garde.

□ 38. Orthodox Church of the Apparition

The Orthodox Church of the Apparition (literally, "of the Sign") is a Russian Orthodox church in the city of Vilnius. The church was restored by Russian Government in 2005-2006.

□ 39. Bust of Gaon Elijahu

Address: 4A Žydų gatvė, Vilnius 01131, Lithuania

The Bust in the center of the plazza, called "Howling Lions", was created by sculptor A. Glinkas. The statue is dedicated to the Vilna Gaon (Elijah ben Solomon Zalman) - one of the greatest Talmudists of all times, famous for his deep learning and genius.

□ 40. Church of St. Francis and St. Bernard

Address: Maironio gatvé 10, Vilnius, Lithuania
Phone: +370 8 616 01159
Email: info@bernardinai.lt
Web: http://parapija.bernardinai.lt/

The Church of St. Francis and St. Bernard was constructed between 1387 and 1416 by Grand Duke Vytautas as a family church for the Gediminid dynasty. In particular, the altarpiece carved by Master Alojzy for Vytautas' funeral has survived to date. This is one of only a few examples of Lithuanian Gothic art. Its interior also includes a pulpit cast in copper made in 1582 in Vilnius, one of the earliest works of this kind in Lithuania.

☐ 41. Antakalnis Cemetery

Address: 12 Karių Kapų gatvė, Vilnius 10313, Lithuania

This famous cemetery is the final resting place for many Lithuanian patriots, as well as professional and political leaders. The cemetery is particularly noted for the burials of the Great Seimas parliament members of Lithuania and Polish insurrectionist Tadeusz Kosciuszko. Additionally, a mass grave site for Soviet victims of the KGB's Vilnius operation in 1956 was established at Antakalnis Cemetery in 1992. Antakalnis Cemetery serves as both a memorial and a tourist attraction.

☐ 42. Adam Mickiewicz Memorial

Address: 9 Maironio gatvė, Vilnius 01124, Lithuania

The Adam Mickiewicz Monument in Vilnius is a monument in the vicinity of the Saint Anne's Church and the Bernardine Monastery, by Maironio Street along the shores of the Neris River. It was erected in 1896-97 (designed by sculptor Giuseppe David – famous for his monument to Nicolaus Copernicus) on occasion of the 100th anniversary of the birth of the Polish writer Adam Mickiewicz and is a copy of a sculpture erected in Krakow.

☐ 43. Chiune Sugihara Sakura Park

Address: Vilnius 08001, Lithuania

Walking over the Japanese Bridge and into Sakura Park, you almost instantly feel like you've found a small piece of Japan in Lithuania. The park is home to hundreds of cherry blossom trees that form a truly stunning sight, as they literally seem to completely cover the green grass in between them. There are plenty of benches around where it's easy to sit down and take it all in or perhaps write a message on one of the cherry blossom petals that have fallen onto the floor.

☐ 44. Lithuanian National Opera and Ballet Theatre

Address: A. Vienuolio gatvé 1, Vilnius, Lithuania
Phone: +370 5 262 07 27
Email: info@opera.lt
Web: https://www.opera.lt/

The Lithuanian National Opera and Ballet Theatre in Vilnius is one of the oldest opera houses in the Baltics. In its early years, it was also the home of the struggling Lithuanian Grand Duke's Theatre, which was formed in 1920. Subsequently, it saw a continuous growth in popularity and stature, and became one of the most important venues for opera, ballet and plays on the Baltic region. It is also here that several famous operas have been premiered, including Vytautas Klova's 'Pilėnai'.

☐ 45. Mindaugas Bridge

Address: Mindaugo tiltas, Vilnius 01013, Lithuania

The Mindaugas Bridge is a physical connection between the districts of Žirmūnai and Old Town. It also serves as a metaphorical link between past and present, as well as between two cultures – Lithuanians and Poles. The bridge is decorated with dolphins which resemble playful children and symbolise Vilnius citizens' joy at the city's rebirth. The sculptor Povilas Budrys created characters out of glass fibre-reinforced concrete that has been covered by bronze casting, and every dolphin even gets its own name.

☐ 46. Steinberg Planetarium

Address: Konstitucijos gatvé 12a, Vilnius, Lithuania
Phone: +370 8 52 724 148
Email: planet@itpa.lt
Web: http://planetarium.tfai.vu.lt/

Steinberg Planetarium was the first planetarium in the Baltic States. It is located in the Vilnius University Astronomical Observatory.

Look at millions of stars, explore constellations, planets, nebulae and galaxies in the space theater hall. In total darkness under a 10-meter dome you can see the sky full of shooting stars and listen to interesting stories about the Universe.

☐ 47. House of the Signatories

Address: Pilies gatvé 26, Vilnius, Lithuania
Phone: (8 ~ 5) 231 44 37
Email: signataru.namai@lnm.lt

The House of the Signatories was built in 1640 and was originally named Bernardine's House. In 1679 the lot belonged to Jan Sapiega, Field Hetman of Lithuania, who rebuilt it and then sold it to the Bernardine monks in 1715. The building underwent major architectural changes in 1825 by Joachim Hryszkiewicz. The House of the Signatories received its present name after Lithuania became independent, on February 16, 1918. On that day, twenty members of the Council of Lithuania voted for independence, which then went into effect on November 28, 1918.

□ 48. Vichy Vandens Park

Address: Ozo gatvé 14, Vilnius, Lithuania
Web: https://www.vandensparkas.lt/

The Vichy Vandens Park, Vilnius is a stunning aqua park located in the green territory near the River Neris and Lake Galverena. This stylish aqua park is a wonderland of grounds consisting of cafes, pools and saunas. It offers a unique Polynesian atmosphere with waterfalls, streams and luxurious villas. This place is ideal for corporate parties, birthdays, weddings, stag nights or for spending some time with your loved ones.

□ 49. Freedom Tile

Address: 2 Katedros aikštė, Vilnius 01143, Lithuania

The symbol of freedom, a tile with the word 'VILNIUS' written across it, was placed on Adam Mickiewicz Alley in 1960, where you may find it today between the Bell Tower and the Cathedral.

Also known as the Miracle Tile or Freedom Tile, if you happen to pass by it, step on it and make a wish.

52

☐ 50. Lithuanian National Drama Theatre

Address: Gedimino prospektas 4, Vilnius, Lithuania
Phone: 8 618 75 780
Email: info@teatras.lt
Web: http://www.teatras.lt/

The Lithuanian National Drama Theatre is one of the most prominent publicly funded performing arts venues and cultural institutions in Lithuania. In the early 2000s a major revitalisation programme was undertaken to replace the 1960s premises with state-of-the-art performance spaces, which were opened in 2011. The façade of the theatre is adorned by the impressive brass sculpture by Romas Miestanavičius titled "The Feast of Muses".

□ 51. St. Ignatius Church

The Church of St. Ignatius is a Catholic Church that serves as the cathedral of the military in Lithuania. It is located in the heart of Vilnius Old Town. Its historic structure belongs to 16th century Renaissance style while the current appearance – 1885-89 by architect who was inspired by Notre Dame in Paris, is neo-Gothic and neo-Romanesque.

□ 52. Europos Parkas

Address: Serbentų gatvė, Skirgiškės 15013, Lithuania

Phone: +370 5 2377 077

Email: hq@europosparkas.lt

Discover the 50-hectare, open-air museum Europos Parkas, with its impressive sculptures at the "center of Europe". The museum is located 17 kilometres from Vilnius and a visit will immerse you in Lithuanian and international modern art.

☐ 53. Vileišis Palace

Address: 6 Antakalnio gatvė, Vilnius 10308, Lithuania

The Vileišis Palace is the best representative of neo-baroque architecture in Lithuania. Construction began in 1904 at the behest of its owner, Duke Petras Vileišis. The complex was designed by R. Madaus and features a balance between modernity and historical tradition. The Palace was built from red brick as a local interpretation or Vilnius baroque with Neo-Gothic and Neo-Renaissance elements. In the front part, there are two medieval columns salvaged from the Old Town Hall of Vilnius (demolished in 1865).

☐ 54. Radziwiłł Palace

Address: 24 Vilniaus gatvė, Vilnius 01402, Lithuania

Built for Mikołaj Krzysztof "the Black" Radziwiłł between 1592–1597, the palace was designed by a famous Italian architect Michelangelo Palloni. Following the death of its last owners in 1782, it was rented to Karl Friedrich von Rumohr who sold it to the tsarist government of Imperial Russia in 1832. The palace housed the Vilnius Governor General and later - the Russian Tsar's official representative Alexander Karlovich Giers. In 1866 some of its interiors were remodeled into a more luxurious style.

□ 55. Energy and Technology Museum

Address: Rinktinės gatvé 2, Vilnius, Lithuania
Phone: +37052782085
Email: info@emuziejus.lt
Web: http://www.emuziejus.lt/

The Museum of Energy and Technology is located in the cellar of the former Vilnius power station. It begins with an exhibition of energetics and tells the story of energy as a means of human civilization development and progress. Special spaces are dedicated to the emergence and development of the electric car, and its key role in our way of life.

□ 56. Vilnius Gediminas Technical University

Web: https://www.vgtu.lt/

The Gediminas Technical University is the leading technological institution in Lithuania. This multi-disciplined institute has been at the forefront of research and academic studies for more than 60 years. The university's 11 faculties are all highly regarded for their work in their respective fields and offer a large variety of degree programs.

□ 57. Rokantiškės Castle Ruins

Address: Naujoji Vilnia 11001, Lithuania

Rokantiškės is the ruins of a medieval castle in Vilnius. The area was first mentioned in written sources in 1465 as the town of Palksniunen or Palkuny. It was destroyed during the Swedish invasion of 1655–1661, but rebuilt afterwards. It was destroyed again during the Great Northern War (1700–1721) and ruined during the reign of Peter I of Russia.

☐ 58. Panorama Shopping Mall

Address: Saltoniškių gatvé 9, Vilnius, Lithuania
Phone: +370 5 219 58 11
Web: http://www.panorama.lt/en

Visit the gigantic shopping mecca called Panorama. It features a wide selection including electronics, clothing and accessories, food courts and supermarkets, as well as a cinema.

☐ 59. Kairėnai Manor

Address: 47 Kairėnų gatvė, Vilnius 10007, Lithuania

Kairėnai Manor is famous for its graveyard as it is the final resting place of many important figures in Lithuanian history. The owners of the manor also invited outstanding artists, architects and craft-workers to work here, making Kairėnai a cultural centre. Furthermore, an outstanding example of early Baroque art can be found in the manor's chapel and one of the first parks in Lithuania has been reconstructed within the territory.

Picture Credits

Vilnius, Lithuania Cover: DominikaKukulka / 5068706 (Pixabay)

St. Anne's Church: Pierre Andre Leclercq (GFDL)

Vilnius Cathedral: Bernt Rostad (CC BY 2.0)

Vilnius Town Hall: Facemepls (CC BY 2.0)

The Hill of the Three Crosses: Rimantas Lazdynas (CC-BY-SA-3.0)

Gediminas Tower: Bernt Rostad (CC BY 2.0)

Vilniaus Street: Algirdas (CC-BY-SA-3.0)

St Catherine's Church: Diliff (CC BY-SA 3.0)

Artillery Bastion: Alma Pater (CC BY-SA 3.0)

Angel of Užupis: Facemepls (CC BY 2.0)

Literatu Street Artwork: Modris Putns (CC BY-SA 3.0)

Museum of Occupations and Freedom Fights: Bernt Rostad (CC BY 2.0)

Bernardine Garden: Pofka (CC BY-SA 3.0)

Egg: Elias Bizannes (CC BY-SA 2.0)

Tauras Hill: Facemepls (CC BY 2.0)

Church of St. Peter & St. Paul: Wojsyl (CC-BY-SA-3.0)

Upper Castle: Rimantas Lazdynas (CC BY-SA 3.0)

Basilian Gates: Alma Pater (PD)

Vilnius University: Mantas Indrašius (CC BY-SA 2.5)

White Bridge: Bernt Rostad (CC BY 2.0)

Pilies Street: Marcin Białek (GFDL)

Orthodox Church of the Holy Spirit: Chad Kainz (CC BY 2.0)

St. Johns' Church: Diliff (CC BY-SA 3.0)

Rasu Cemetery: Arz (PD)

King Mindaugas Memorial: Facemepls (CC BY 2.0)

Jewish Museum: Alma Pater (CC BY-SA 3.0)

Frank Zappa Memorial: Adam Jones (CC BY-SA 2.0)

Gediminas Hill: Averater (CC BY-SA 3.0)

Vingis Park: Umnik (PD)

Bernardinai Cemetery: Foma (CC-BY-SA-3.0)

National Museum of Lithuania: Julius (CC BY 2.5)

Verkiai Palace: Robis (CC-BY-SA-3.0)

Vilnius Art Museum: (CC-BY-SA-3.0)

TV Tower: Facemepls (CC BY 2.0)

Geographical midpoint of Europe: Rimantas Lazdynas (CC-BY-SA-3.0)

Orthodox Church of the Apparition: Loraine90 (CC BY-SA 3.0)

Bust of Gaon Elijahu: Julius (CC BY 2.5)

Church of St. Francis and St. Bernard: Juliux (CC BY-SA 3.0)

Antakalnis Cemetery: Kontis Šatūnas (PD)

Lithuanian National Opera and Ballet Theatre: Qwarc (CC-BY-SA-3.0)

Mindaugas Bridge: Tak.Wing (CC BY-SA 2.0)

Steinberg Planetarium: Stefan Didam (CC BY-SA 3.0)

House of the Signatories: Julius (CC BY 2.5)

St. Ignatius Church: Loraine (CC BY-SA 4.0)

Europos Parkas: Legionas (CC BY 2.5)

Vileišis Palace: Alma Pater (PD)

Energy and Technology Museum: Rimantas Lazdynas (CC BY-SA 3.0)

Vilnius Gediminas Technical University: Vgtu123 (CC BY-SA 3.0)

Rokantiškės Castle Ruins: Juliux (CC-BY-SA-3.0)

www.ingramcontent.com/pod-product-compliance
Lightning Source LLC
Chambersburg PA
CBHW071449150726
48000CB00006B/2496